Stoicism

Dark Psychology Secrets: A Guide to What You Should Know to Broaden Your Thinking, Develop Confidence, Refine Your Mind, and Embrace True Happiness

TABLE OF CONTENTS

The information in the following pages is broadly considered a truthful and accurate account of facts and as such, any inattention, use, or misuse of the information in question by the reader will render any resulting actions solely under their purview. There are no scenarios in which the publisher or the original author of this work can be in any fashion deemed liable for any hardship or damages that may befall them after undertaking information described herein.

Additionally, the information in the following pages is intended only for informational purposes and should thus be thought of as universal. As befitting its nature, it is presented without assurance regarding its prolonged validity or interim quality. Trademarks that are mentioned are done without written consent and can in no way be considered an endorsement from the trademark holder.

INTRODUCTION

Stoicism might be daunting and boring, and in some instances, might be the last thing that anybody would want to hear or learn about. Many years back, no one would spend much time learning about this topic but as years passed; many have fallen in love and become enthusiastic with the numerous beliefs, principles, virtue, insights about emotions and more.

Stoicism no longer sounds boring today. Instead, this becomes highly relevant and contains powerful tools that individuals can use and take advantage in today's modern and fast-paced world. Stoicism can also be considered as a toolset that helps individuals direct their actions and thoughts in a highly unpredictable world.

If you wish to learn more about stoicism, this eBook is perfect for you. The main goal of this book is to answer a lot of questions like what stoicism is, what is its history, what is its virtue and more.

Chapter 1: Dealing with Negative Emotions

Stoics are capable of managing their emotions pretty well. Some individuals can attest that before they discovered and learn more about stoicism, they were plagued by particular teenage angst that most of the experience. Meditations by Marcus Aurelius also play a part in these experiences.

Though some individuals have not been cured of negative emotions and feelings and still experienced lows, stoicism has given them tools to deal with these. Stoics are individuals who don't give a care to stupid things in the world that many individuals care about. Stoics have emotions but just fir things that do matter in this world. Stoics are one of the most real individuals alive.

Stoic Believes that Life Isn't Easy

When life becomes tough, stoics will not tell you to be happy and cheer up if you are feeling down. They won't tell you to be more positive either. The truth is, they will propagate the opposite. They also believe that you should try having hope for the future but eradicate this instead. For Stoics, hope is a heroine of emotions, and that higher one is lifted, the deeper he will fall.

Stoics would usually tell you something negative will happen, and that includes your partner leaving you, your car being hijacked, ending up in prison and many other bad things. But things will be okay. Stoics would tell you that life is full of misfortunes and you will get through it.

They also declare that negative feelings and emotions are the results of wrong judgments and that individuals expectations for realities weren't correct, and they should live in accordance with the truth or reality.

For the stoics, the good mental condition is identified by its virtue and capacity to reason out. There is this unanimous belief within the stoic community and that individuals should not be driven by emotions but by rationality instead. But this does not necessarily mean stamping out emotions altogether. This means getting rid of emotions out of the driver's seat and positioning them into the passengers' seat.

The belief of living in proper accordance with nature is probably controversial in the hedonistic modernity. This implies that foods are strictly for health and survival and sex, mainly for reproduction. They believed that having material goods will end up possessing them and that the more things you purchased, the higher the level of worrying about maintaining these things.

According to Marcus Aurelius, almost no material is needed for a happier life for one has fully understood existence. Believing in suicide is even more controversial. Stoics believed that a person must be allowed to take his own life.

When Seneca was asked to take his life by committing suicide, he did not even bat an eye. And while his children and wife hold firmly into him crying, he declared calmly that there is no need to cry over aspects of life for the entirety of life calls for these tears.

Seneca once said: "*Can you no longer see a road to freedom? It's right in front of you. You need only turn over your wrists.* "— Seneca

Now that you have learned more about stoics' belief, you might now be wondering how these can be applied in your life. The following information reveals some of the techniques used by stoics.

Stoics Equipment-The Tools in Living a Much Better Life

If you also wanted to live a much better life as you embrace stoicism, the following tools can help you accomplish this:

Negative Visualization

This pertains to the act of imagining the loss of what matters to you. It's often used by stoics to get rid of their fear for loss and to reduce the impacts when a loss happens. If you are that afraid and bothered about losing your spouse, imagine that he or she already left you. In any case, you are also afraid of losing your most valued car; imagine that you have just crashed your vehicle to the pole. If you are worried and afraid of losing money, then imagine living in the streets. And then ask yourself, is this the condition that you fear.

The premise of negative visualization imagines the loss of a lot of things, and when these occur, there will be less emotional impacts. You'll have expected it already for the reason that despite real efforts to avoid bad things, these happen. According to Seneca, misfortune weighs heavily on individuals who expect nothing but good fortunes.

Most individuals have lived in hedonic adaptations wherein they chase their desires only to realize that they have adapted to a new state and have more desires now. Negative visualization tends to reverse the process of hedonic adaptions. Rather than aiming for things that you do not have, negative visualization helps you desire the things that you already have. Visualizing loss of limb, loss of material goods or partner, a particular gratitude towards them.

Stoics asserted that during the time's, individuals are enjoying their loved ones. They need to periodically reflect on possibilities that existence of loved ones will disappear. Epictetus give them a piece of advice that whenever they kiss a child, keep in mind that this child was given to them for present and not inseparably or forever. Individuals should also reflect on possibilities that their fondness and enjoyment with the child are meant to end.

Worry Only on Things that You Can Control

Epictetus proclaimed that the most imperative choice in life is deciding whether to involve and concern yourself with internal and external. Most individuals choose external. They believe that their environment displays what's bad and what's good.

Stoics also believed that all harm and benefits come from within and that individuals should give up the rewards of the external world to achieve freedom, calmness and tranquility. Desire, by default, makes individuals unhappy for the reason that they wanted something that they do not have. The desire and happiness for what's present are impossible. Techniques they've used in managing such unforgiving truth are changing their desires and not the world around them. In order to convince themselves out of the desires in their environments, stoics pronounced that their major desires must be able to prevent frustrations from developing desires that they cannot fulfill.

This idea was illustrated by Epictetus using a model named Dichotomy of Control. This is simple truth forgotten. Some things are really up to us, and certain things are not. Just focus on the things that you are in control.

Offer Yourself into Fate

Most individuals expect for things they want in this world. When these expectations do not come true, it might feel like the universe is not in favor. Stoics advised individuals to take fate or reality as they go along. Epictetus reminded individuals that they are actors in a play that is written by fate. People cannot choose the role they will play so instead of wanting things that did not happen, desire for the events to happen. According to Seneca, it's an excellent consolation that it's together with universe people have swept along.

Marcus Aurelius directed that something else would be defying nature. That individuals should love individuals that the destinies have bestowed upon them, welcome whatever obligations fall into them and acknowledge reality as they go. Remember, this is a similar man who invested most of his energy and effort for wars he needed to fight.

Reflection

Seneca states that individuals ought to intermittently consider the day by day events that have occurred and how they can improve (concurs intensely with the personal growth genre). He obtained this idea from Sextius, his teacher, who announced that he would cross-examine his mind with a similar inquiry:

"What illness of yours have you relieved or cured today? What failing have you stood up to? Where would you be able to demonstrate improvement?" When he was excessively forceful in criticizing somebody, as opposed to proclaiming the individual for being powerless willed or weak-willed, he offered himself guidance. He decided that he somehow happened to give valuable analysis; he shouldn't just consider whether the analysis is substantial as well as think about whether the individual can stand being condemned or criticized.

It would be best to have some time doing some self-reflection taking, for instance, when writing into your diary. Ask yourself what you are grateful for today? How can you have improved today?

We have a long way to learn from stoics. A significant number of their strategies for carrying on with a solid passionate life can be connected every day. Their common sense and well-grounded frame of mind never stop to amaze people.

Emotion Control

People love power and feeling incredible and powerful. They respect stories of fortitude of individuals who face their adversaries and difficulties triumphantly as if they were Hercules. People might want to feel, in the event that they could, as the strong cliff which faces the ferocious seas and oceans without even moving and without giving in even a bit. It's possible. Individuals can encapsulate that control.

Individuals need to see, however, what that power is and how to utilize it. Stoicism is usually represented as a way of thinking or a philosophy with one major aim, and it is suppression or concealment of feeling, prominently accepted. It depicts stoics as a bit of iron or wood, fearless yet emotionless instead. This does not remain constant for Stoicism. Stoics are, toward the day's end, individuals charged with shyness, fear and love and humans to humans. The point of Stoicism isn't to suppress feeling; it is to live admirably well.

Emotion

An emotional condition of cognizance where delight, distress, dread, abhor, or the like, is experienced, as recognized from volitional and psychological conditions and states of consciousness.

There is no chance to get where individuals can't feel the emotion; feelings emerge. On the off chance that you happen to be in the subway amid the night and somebody hauls out a weapon, you will be apprehensive; you can't control not being afraid. Something very similar occurs with each circumstance throughout everyday life. When you have a crucial meeting, you will feel somewhat anxious, and if asking a lady out? Well, you might feel anxious and on edge also.

What Stoics contended with about feelings and emotions is that you don't need to stifle them, but instead, you should act in manners that give you the good ones and dodge the negative ones. You don't need to feel remorseful about feeling angry or afraid. The ascent of feeling is something that isn't under your immediate control. Thus this also turns out to be part of being indifferent.

Indifference means everything that isn't under individuals' immediate control. People must be cautiously mindful of what it is and what isn't that is under their immediate control. Feelings have a dubious impact, since they are the ones feeling it, and they also feel rulers of their emotions since they are feeling them literally. However, they cannot truly control the next emotion of thought that arises. Practicing stoics, in any case, has the limit of applied reasons. Volition is the ability to exert will. It is in the ability to apply own will where one can end up like the unmoving rock amidst the waves. The feeling may rise, yet it is exposed to our reason and cardinal ethics: the knowledge, justice, courage and temperance.

Stoically, individuals can ignore interests as indifferent, yet at the same time, feel the entire circle of feelings and emotions without limitations; it is in this power, where individuals have emotion control.

Ensure that rulings and sovereign piece of your spirit and soul stay unaffected by each movement, violent or smooth, in your flesh and that it doesn't consolidate with them, yet encircles itself, and limits these encounters to bodily parts. At whatever point they communicate themselves into the mind utilizing virtue of the other sympathy, as will undoubtedly happen unified organisms, you shouldn't try resisting the temptations which are considered natural ones. However, you should not allow the ruling center of adding its own and further judgments that experiences are bad or good.

> You can feel dread, yet act with mental fortitude at any rate.
>
> You can feel disgrace and shame, yet stand gladly anyway.
>
> You can feel outraged or anger, yet always act with justice.

Action and stoicism go hand in hand. Stoics don't wait, and he acts no matter what. The more the difficulties, the more noteworthy for the Stoic personality and mind because for this can practice its power of overcoming it.

Epictetus also said:

"*The greater the difficulty, the more glory in surmounting it. Skillful pilots gain their reputation from storms and tempests.* "

Also, the notable difference between a wise man and fool man depends on the power of putting everything that he experiences into a test for his reasons and then act accordingly.

Chapter 2: Spiritual Exercise to Become Stoic

Stoicism is known for some of its central teachings. This sets out to remind individuals that the world out there can be unpredictable. This also tells how instant and short life can be, how strong, steadfast, and in control individuals are of themselves. Finally, individuals' source of discontentment lies on their impulsive dependency in their reflexive senses rather than logic.

Stoicism does not concern itself with complex theories of the world. However, this is more concerned about helping individuals overcome destructive feelings, and then act on what can be acted upon. This is built for actions and not really on endless debates.

Stoicism has three known principal leaders: Marcus Aurelius, the Roman Empire's emperor who sat down every day to write notes regarding restraints, humility, and compassion. Another leader is Epictetus who endured all the horrors of the slavery founding his school, wherein he taught many of the greatest minds of Rome. The last one is Seneca. When Seneca was demanded to commit suicide, he only thinks about comforting his friends and of course, his wife. Stoicism is being practiced by presidents, kings, entrepreneurs, writers, artists, and more. Both modern and historical men describe stoicism as a way of life. But stoicism differs from many of the existing schools in one significant aspect. This aspect is its purpose, which is said to be a practical application. It isn't an utterly intellectual enterprise.

Stoicism is also a tool that individuals can use to be better in any particular craft, be better with friends, and most of all, become people. Moreover, stoics are known to practice these so-called spiritual exercises where they drew their strength from every day.

- **Practice Misfortune**

Seneca suggests that individuals need to set aside a particular number of days every month and practice poverty. Wear the worst clothes, eat little food and go out and leave the comforts of their home. Individuals need to put themselves face to face with wants. Seneca said that this would probably make individuals asked themselves "*is this really what they dread?*" Remember, this is an activity or exercise and not an expository device. He doesn't really "consider "misfortune," he means live it. Comfort is the most exceedingly awful sort of slavery since you're always apprehensive that a person or thing will take this. On the off chance that you can't just anticipate but rather practice misfortune, then at that point, chance loses its capacity of disrupting your life.

Montaigne was hooked with an old drinking game where the individuals take their turns in holding up corpse painting inside the coffin and then cheered: "*Drink and be happy for when you are dead, you will resemble this.*"

Emotions such as fear and anxiety have their foundations in vulnerability and once in a while in the experience. Any individual who has made a significant bet on himself knows the level of energy the two states can expend. The ideal solution is doing something regarding ignorance. Make yourself more acquainted with the things, the most pessimistic situations that you're anxious about.

Practice what you are afraid of whether the simulation of mind or maybe in real life. The drawback is always transient and reversible.

- **Train Perception to Prevent Bad or Good**

Marcus Aurelius, you need to choose not being hurt or feeling armed. Do not feel harmed and you have not been.

The Stoics had an activity called "Turning the Obstacle Upside Down." What they intended to do was make it difficult not to practice the art of way thinking or philosophy. Supposing that you can appropriately flip around an issue, each "awful" issue turns into a new source of a positive one.

Assume for a second that you are attempting to support somebody, and they react by being reluctant to collaborate. Rather than making your life progressively troublesome, the activity says, they're guiding you to new virtues. Examples of this would be persistence or understanding, or the demise of somebody near you, or an opportunity to express fortitude.

Marcus Aurelius described this as an impediment to action. The thing that comes in the way becomes the way.

It must sound familiar since it is a similar intuition behind the teachable moments of Obama. Before the election, Joe Klein asked Obama how he'd settled on his choice to respond to Reverend Wright embarrassment. He said that the best thing to do is not damage control; it was to address Americans like adults. And what he wound up doing was transforming an adverse circumstance into the ideal stage for his speech regarding the race.

One of the common holdbacks about entrepreneurs is that they exploit, even make opportunities. To the Stoic, everything is an opportunity. The Reverend Wright outrage, a baffling situation where your assistance goes neglected, the passing of a friend or family member, none of those are considered opportunities in the typical sense of the word. They are the opposites. They are hindrances. What a Stoic does is transform obstacles to opportunities.

There's no bad or good to practicing stoics only perception, and you can't control this perception. You can opt to extrapolate your very first impressions. If you are tied into your first response into dispassion, you will find things to be only opportunities.

- **Keep in Mind-It is All Ephemeral**

Marcus Aurelius has written effective and simple reminder to help him in staying balanced and regaining perspective.

Rundown the list of individuals who felt serious outrage at something: the most popular, the most grievous, the most hated, and the most whatever. Where's all at this point? Dust, legend... or not by any means a legend. Think about all the examples. What's more, how trivial the things individuals need so enthusiastically are.

It is critical to take note of that 'passion' here isn't the advanced usage individuals are comfortable and familiar with as in thinking about something or enthusiasm. As Don Robertson clarifies in his book, when the Stoics talk about defeating passions at which they called patheiai, they allude into the irrational, excessive, and unhealthy emotions and desires. Anger is an excellent sample or model. This is a vital piece to recall: to replace them with patheiai such as joy rather than excessive pleasure.

Coming back into the point of the activity, it's basic: recall how little you are and for the matter, also recall how small most things are. Keep in mind that accomplishments can somewhat be ephemeral and that your ownership of them if only for a moment.

In the case, everything seems ephemeral, what matters really? The present time matters. Being a decent individual and making the best choice at present, that is the thing that really matters, and that is what was essential to the Stoics.

Taking, for instance, Alexander the Great who vanquished the known world and had urban communities and cities named after him to show respect and honor. This is a widely known or common knowledge. The Stoics would likewise bring up that, one time while drunk, Alexander got into a fight with his dearest companion and friend Cleitus and killed him accidentally. Eventually, he was down and out to the point that he couldn't drink or eat for three days. Critics were brought from all over Greece to perceive what could be done about his despondency, without much of any result.

Is this the characteristic of an effective and successful life? From a personal viewpoint, it makes a just a little different if your name is embellished on a guide in case that you lose perspectives and you hurt everyone around you.

Learn from the mistake of Alexander. Be aware, honest, and humble. This is something that you can have every day of your life. You do not need to fear somebody taking it from you or, more regrettable still, and it is taking control over you.

- **Taking View from Above**

The words of Marcus Aurelius go like this:

How delightfully Plato had put it. At whatever point you need to discuss about individuals, it's ideal for taking bird's-eye view and being able to see everything at the same time—of social events, , weddings and separations, births, death, quiet spaces, noisy rooms, each foreign individuals, occasions, commemorations, advertises—combined altogether and orchestrated in a matching of contraries.

It suggests people make a stride back, zoom out, and then see life from a much higher point than their own. This activity-thinking about all individuals and prompt people to take perspectives and just only like the past exercise, remind them how little they are. It reorients people, and as a Stoic researcher, Pierre Hadot put it, view from above changes one's worth decisions on things such as power, luxury and all the stresses and worries from day to day life become so ridiculous. Perceiving how little you are in the grand scheme of things is just one aspect of this exercise. The second progressively unobtrusive point is taking advantage of what the Stoics call as mutual interdependence or sympatheia, or a common reliance with the entire of humankind.

As the space traveler Edgar Mitchell, one of the very first people to encounter a genuine 'see from above' place it. In space, you build up instant worldwide awareness, individuals' orientation, intense disappointment or dissatisfaction with the condition of the world, and an impulse to take care of business. Take some steps back from your very own worries and concerns help yourself to remember your obligation to other people.

- **Memento Mori-Meditating on Your Mortality**

Seneca asked to give individuals the chance to set up their brains as though they have reached the end of life. Give people a chance to defer nothing. Give them the chance to adjust life's books every day. The person who puts in the finishing touches their life every day will never be short of time.

The statement from Seneca above removes a portion of Memento Mori—the antiquated routine with regards to reflections particularly on mortality that returns to Socrates, who said that the best possible routine with regards to theory is *"tied in with nothing else except being dead or dying."* In Marcus Aurelius' Meditations, he wrote that *"You could leave life at this moment."* Give that a chance to figure out what you do and what you think and say. That was a reminder for every individual to keep carrying on and living a life of virtues at the present moments. Do not wait.

Thinking about your mortality is possibly discouraging on the off chance that you overlook the main issue. The Stoics discover this idea humbling and invigorating. It is no longer surprising that one of Seneca's life stories is entitled Dying Every Day. It is Seneca who asked individuals to let themselves know "You may not get up tomorrow," when going to bed and you may not rest or sleep as well when waking up as tokens of mortality. Or then again as another Stoic, Epictetus, asked his students to keep exile death before their eyes every day, alongside everything that appears to be awful-thusly, you will never have an idea nor have unnecessary want. Use those updates and contemplate them day by day-letting them be the essential building blocks of carrying on with your life without limits and not wasting even for just a second.

- **Is This Really Within my Control**

According to Epictetus, the main task in life is identifying as well as separating matters so it can be said clearly to one's self which externals are under his control and which ones have to do with choices that he can control. Where should one look for evil and good? Not to the uncontrollable essentials but for his or her externals.

The absolute most significant practice in the Stoic way of thinking and philosophy is separating between what they can change and what they can't; including what they have an impact over and what they don't. A flight has been delayed or cancelled because of the weather-no measure of yelling and getting angry at the agent will end the storm.

No exact amount of saying your wish will make you shorter or taller in a different nation. Regardless of how hard you attempt, you can't make somebody like you. What's more, time spent flinging yourself at these steady items is a time not spent on things you can change.

Come back to this inquiry day by day—in each trying circumstance. Use a journal and think about it always. In the event that you can concentrate on clarifying what parts of your day are actually within your control and the parts that are not, you'll not just be happier. You'll have special advantages over others who fail to understand that they're fighting battles they cannot win.

- **Journal**

Epictetus is known as the slave. Marcus Aurelius is the ruler, Seneca the power agent and dramatist. These three men led drastically different lives. Be that as it may, they appeared to share one propensity for all intents and purpose: Journaling.

In some structure, every one of them did it. It might be Epictetus who reprimands his students that particular way of thinking and was something they should "record step by step," that his writings were the manner by which they "should practice themselves. During evening is Seneca's most preferred time to journal.

At the point when obscurity had fallen, and his significant other went asleep, he disclosed to a companion and said that he looks at his whole day and return over what he had done and stated, concealing nothing from himself and passing nothing. Then he would hit the bed and find that the sleep that follows and pursues this self-examination was especially sweet. Furthermore, Marcus, he was the most fabulous among journalers, and people are fortunate enough that his works get by to them.

In Stoicism, journaling is more than some straightforward diary. This day by day, practice is considered the philosophy. Get ready for the day ahead. Consider the day that has passed. Helping oneself to remember the knowledge he has gained from his educators, from reading and from his encounters and experiences.

It's insufficient to hear these exercises once. Instead, one practices them again and again, turns them over in their own mind, and above all, thinks of them down and feels them coursing through their fingers in doing as such. Along these lines, journaling is Stoicism. It's practically difficult to have one of the other is absent.

- **Negative Visualization Practices**

The premeditation of evil or the premeditation Malorum is a particular exercise in Stoicism that includes imagining many things that can go wrong or that can be taken away from you. This exercise helps in preparing you for inevitable setbacks in life.

Individuals don't often get what is rightfully theirs, regardless of whether they have earned it. Not all things are as perfect and direct as they might suspect they might be. Psychologically, individuals should set themselves up for this to occur. It is one of the most dominant exercises in the Stoics' toolbox to build strength and resilience.

Seneca, for example, would start by means of reviewing and practicing his solid plans say, for instance, traveling. And after that, in his mind or in journaling as mentioned above, he would go over the things that could turn out badly or keep it from occurring - a storm could emerge, the chief could become sick, pirates could assault the ship.

By doing this negative visualization, one can be prepared and work that disruption to his plans. One can also be fitted for victory or defeat.

- **Amor Fati or Love and Embrace Everything that Happens**

A well-known German logician and philosopher Friedrich Nietzsche would portray his equation for human significance as love fati or affection or love for destiny. That one needs nothing to be considered unique or something else, not advance, not in reverse, not until forever. Not simply tolerate what is vital, still hides it and love it.

The Stoics knew about this frame of mind and attitude, and stoics really embraced it. 2,000 years ago, while Marcus Aurelius is writing in his very own diary which became widely popular and recognized as Meditations, Aurelius would say that a bursting fire makes fire and brilliance out of everything that is tossed into it. Another Stoic, Epictetus, who as a disabled slave has confronted many adversities, said that you should not expect things to happen the way you wanted them to happen. Wish that the things that happen occur the way it should happen then you will be surely happy.

It is for this reason that love fati is Stoic mindset and exercise that you can take on to make the best out of whatever occurs: Treating every single minute— regardless of how hard it is as something to be fully embraced and not to be avoided. To not exclusively approve of it, however, cherish it and be fine with it. With the goal that is like oxygen to a flame, impediments and difficulty become fuel for your real potential.

Chapter 3: Stoicism and Christianity

Most individuals see Christianity and Stoicism being polar opposites. However, belief systems overlap in various ways. Though there are more differences than similarities that exist between Christianity and Stoicism, individuals should not let this preclude them from thinking about what school of philosophy provides as ultimate answers to a perennial question "*how should we really live*?"

Stoicism, the Greek way of thinking and philosophy framed in Athens, discovered its following when the Greek world was in disorder. Alexander the Great died at a young age after the entirety of his victories, and Greece was left fumbling. Offering peace, harmony, and security amid savagery and violence, Stoics know that they can find real happiness by depending on their internal identity or what they call as inner self. They believed that virtue, the highest good, depends on information and that the shrewd can live amicability with the perfect and most divine reason which permeates nature.

Christianity, in view of the lessons of Jesus of Nazareth, teaches empathy, love, charity, forgiveness, and compassion. Like Stoicism, it rose during times of chaos and offered a security and harmony that could prompt joy. The connection has its deep foundation in Jesus as God's physical manifestation. According to Christianity, it is just through Jesus that individuals can get eternal salvation. People spare themselves by means of grace rather than works, while forgiveness of their sins is through faith alone.

Stoicism and Christianity-Similarities

Logos is the Greek term for words. About 500 years before the birth of Jesus, Heraclitus, a Greek philosopher, utilized logos to clarify what he saw as the all-inclusive power of reason that is considered to govern everything. He reveals that all words occur based on the Logos. This conviction turned as Stoicism's great foundation. Jews that speak Greek came to see the Logos as a power sent by God. In John's Gospel, Jesus is recognized as the Word, and this was made flesh and has dwelt among people. He is also the powerful driving force sent by God. Between Christianity and Stoicism, both are said to be monotheistic. Stoicism is known to follow Heraclitus and has faith in a Logos; Christianity is known to follow Jesus and expects followers to have faith in a true God and ensure not to have other except Him. Also, both Christianity and Stoicism serve the Logos/God's will. They teach people that they can free themselves from anxiety and fear by means of submitting to Divine's will.

Also, both Christianity and Stoicism raise a question like, "what or who does an individual serving?" All one does depend on the appropriate response. Instead of being a slave or captive to other people, both Christianity and Stoicism include evolving from concentrating on the self to a self-established one serving God. Matthew 6:24 reveals that it is difficult to worship two divine beings at once. Reverence for one feeds hatred for the other. Therefore, one can't worship money and God or God and individuals' feelings and opinions. Serving oneself is more focused on external appearance; serving God within is expected to break the chains of subjugation to public opinions and empowers followers to look only for good.

At long last, both Christianity and Stoicism look for simplicity in faith and in worship. If worship tends to be showy, it might mean an individual needs other people to notice him, which serves the outside self instead of inner God. Matthew 6:6 states, *"If you pray, go into your room, close the door and pray to your Father, who is unseen. Then, your Father, who sees what is done in secret, will reward you."*

Stoicism and Christianity-Differences

As for the contrasts between Christianity and Stoicism, Stoicism at certain extent easier than the last since it has no trinity or demons and holy angels. Besides, in Stoicism, the Logos is a mysterious power while, in Christianity, the Word (Logos) was made flesh and has dwelt among individuals. For the Stoics, an association with the Logos is intellectual, distant, and dependent on ideas of prudence and duty. In Christianity, the relationship with Logos is considerably more personal. It teaches and encourages that God needs their praise, love, and adoration and are even more willing to die for it. Another huge difference between the two is Christians seek God to ask for assistance, while the Stoics look for help from within. Through the petition, Christians request to be discharged from affliction, healed from illness and consoled when in sorrow and distress. On the other hand, Stoicism tells individuals that in the event that if they want good, they have to get it themselves. No soul will assuage them from torments.

Christianity and Stoicism have contending views about human instinct and nature too. For the Stoics, nature has imparted individuals with the ability to reason, which they can practice to live out upright, obedient lives. On the other hand, Christians believed that individuals are brought into the world with a unique sin, which has tainted their inner moral compass. It is just by the finesse of God that individuals are improved and spared. On the other side, the Stoics saw the rational handicap as damaged, while in Christianity, they are seen as children of God deserving of respect and love.

Christianity and stoicism likewise have separating perspectives about the afterlife. In Christianity, the world is viewed as a sad remnant of the world yet to come. Toward the end of time, the dead will rise, Christ will come back to separate the goats from the sheep, and the Kingdom of God will be set up on Earth.

On the other hand, the Stoics made little notice of afterlife and were skeptic about what, in the event that anything lies past the grave. For Stoics, what makes a difference isn't so much of what could conceivably occur after death, yet how individuals utilize the time, they have now.

The expression "God helps individuals who help themselves" pleasantly combines Christianity and stoicism, providing the best of the two worlds. Rather than interminably arguing about which perspective rules, take components that you appreciate in the two customs while developing a way of thinking about how to live, and show that two heads are superior to one.

How Stoicism Really Influenced Christianity

Before Christianity, it cannot be denied that there was already Stoicism, an ancient and unique Greek philosophy with tenets like monotheism and believes a rational plan for the Universe. This is anticipated Christian theology in various ways.

Philo of Alexandria is known to be born in 20 BC and died in AD 50—so the life of Jesus Christ was covered by his period. Philo is a fascinating figure, a Jew having a Greek name, and part of the "Hellenized" Judaism world.

He studied philosophies and also studied more about Plato and Aristotle and, obviously, a faithful and committed student of the Old Testament. In his writings and compositions, there has been an attempt to incorporate methodically the idea of the real Greek logicians and philosophers as well as scriptural truths of the Old Testament.

To become a Hellenized Jew at the time of Jesus Christ's life is actually among the different considerations to become a scholar-somebody who has maybe gone to Athens, yet who in any case has respected the thoughts being imparted and taught deeply in Athens as the pinnacle of philosophical intelligence or wisdom.

Indeed, even in Philo's time, Athens has remained the most brilliant spot on each scholar's guide map. Once there, visiting scholar sees not simply classical architecture and statues. One likewise inhales the vapors and hears the resonance of that celebrated yet long bygone time now.

The schools in Athens remain the best. Alexandria has an incredible library, and it is basically a good center for research, far less piece of the living and long discussion directed with life in Athens at that very time.

Presently, when the early Jewish Christian start the development of what will be known as Christianity, their interests are inside a thoughtfully focused setting that incorporates Stoicism at its core.

Establishment of the Christian Faith

St. Paul delivers his letters to individuals in the huge Roman world as he makes a trip from jurisdiction to jurisdiction. He will go up against not just individuals whose practices differ broadly, whose own theological conviction and local or native ideas are sorts that one could never have found in Athens or even in Rome, yet in addition, the individuals who have created and refined knowledge and philosophical modernity presently through studying Athens.

It isn't surprising then that the one attribute of early Christian teaching is its transparent desire to set up the articles of faith, as these were the lessons of the "genuine religion" in the foundation that it's mentally fulfilling, intellectually rich, and very convincing. Therefore, it isn't astounding that in Paul's very own works, one will discover thoughts taken from Stoic teaching. He was clearly presented to it in his local Tarsus, and it was voiced without attribution on his common natural world as well as its order. In this way, influences of Stoic are apparent in his treatment of someone's faith and belief in God being natural inclination and of beliefs, unlike the theory of affinities of stoics.

In reality, that Stoicism was perceived as maybe the worthiest enemy is obvious from the contentions of the early leaders and fathers of the churches against such thoughts as the physicality of God. The continuing battle against pagan notions will draw out a portion of discerning components in the early Christian way of thinking and philosophy as delivered by certain figures as Origen and Tertullian, the previous referring to Zeno and to Cleanthes positively.

Stoicism-Bridging Philosophy and Faith

There have been debates and debts that were productive and inevitable. The early Fathers of the congregation or the church needed to reconcile the church's teachings, the message found in the life of Christ himself, with philosophies respected and recognized as one of the incredible accomplishments of human idea, regardless of whether if its pagan thought.

Therefore, there should not be an unbridgeable separation between lessons of philosophies and lessons of faith, and these two are desperately incompatible. So there's much intellectual energy committed to having philosophical light offered as a powerful influence for the authority of faith. Given the authentic historical period where these improvements are occurring, it's a Stoic way of thinking that must give the bridge or significant planks of the bridge at least, which leads to Christianity's central tenets. Consider then a portion of Stoicism's features that may have been declared at the time of the Jewish Christians, as these may be consolidated into Philo's writings and others, seeing a mission like the one Philo had set for himself. Presently, there are evident purposes of similarity, yet additionally, issue zones that must be managed.

To begin with, the Stoics and for the Stoics, regardless, what may be known as the Lord of the Stoics is anything but an individual is worried about human welfare in that capacity, however, an amazing "divine fire," working through material and physical methods or modes of operations. Nevertheless, this power or force is normal in its fundamental nature and tends to be immortal. Presently, in this record, the defining highlight of the universe's creative power is its rationality and inexhaustibility.

Stoicism provides undeniable evidence for this- consider just the legitimateness of cosmos itself. In Stoic teaching, especially later Stoic teachings and knowledge of this sort of divine influence is one of the very previously established inclinations that a rational individual is.

This is a significant point. Review the claim of Aristotle that if the craft of shipbuilding were on the wood, they have delivered by nature. All things considered, what the Stoics can get from this notion of concepts of the divine being part of their highly intuitive resources. Such belief in being the type of built in, what they are getting is a rational being recognizing lawfulness and orderliness of cosmos should match up with no further deliberations, in addition to the notion of certain rational agencies behind this. You won't get anything of this kind accidentally.

Chapter 4: Stoic Inner Peace

Inner peace is an intrinsic part of stoicism. Learning more about stoic inner peace can give you clearer insights as to what inner peace is really all about and also learn how controlling your thinking can give you inner peace and more.

Controlling Your Thinking Gives You Inner Peace

Individuals are blessed with an amazing gift-the capacity to be aware of their own reasoning and thinking. You are probably one of those given with this gift, so how do you really take advantage of this blessing? When individuals are unaware of what is going through their mind, they are surrendering control of their mind to the old patterns and habits or propensities that they have made in their lives and giving themselves a chance to keep running on autopilot.

Another part of gaining control overthinking is being aware of thinking. Meditation is about this thought of being aware of thoughts and ideas running through your brain. Few people believe that meditation is clearing the mind, and though it's one form of meditation. Its primary purpose is slowing down enough to make you more aware of your thoughts. If you can see your thoughts, you can look at these dispassionately or objectively and begin to ask yourself, "*how is concentrating on this helps you become a better person?*"

When you do start to see your reasoning and thinking, be mindful so as not to pass judgment on yourself when you do think adversely. See that it's an idea you are having and that you have the alternative of what you need to do with it. You can choose if that thought is one that serves you or not. However, remember that it's only an idea.

In case sitting with your thoughts is hard for you, try sitting down and writing out your thoughts, or you can get your telephone to begin a voice memo and record your contemplations and your thoughts for a couple of minutes. Try not to stress over the saying or the writing that says "right" things, get them out when they come into your head with the goal that you can watch them later. When you have them out of your head, at that point, you can begin to see where you may be unknowingly concentrating on things that are not serving you. You can choose just to let them go. You can also tell your brain that you see thoughts, and it is just fine to let them go. There will be no judgments, only observations.

Figuring out how to improve the nature of your thinking is something that anybody can do. The more you can restrict your distractions, notice your reasoning and slow down, and use reasoned and non-thinking to concentrate only on valuable thoughts. You clear most of the negative mental chatters. If you can calm down the clamor, you can train your mind to establish thinking that encourages you to achieve inner peace and remain more focus on tasks at hand.

The Stoic-The 3 Principles to Keep You Calm During Chaos

Observing individuals living a creative life can help you identify key elements of real expertise, passion, and understanding. What is simple to overlook in that inner system within a person: the set of essential principles governing their behavior and mind.

The moment failure ensues or in times that they need to fully adapt is deemed necessary, how does a person respond. What does he tell himself? What's his philosophy?

Philosophy does not just teach us ways to live well and be better human beings, but this also helps in overcoming tribulations and trials in life. Some schools of thought opt for more debates, and abstract thinking wherein others are ideal tools that are instantly practical into their present undertakings.

The Stoicism's principles are probably the most practical and relevant sets of given rules for the entrepreneurs, artist, and writers of all kinds. Stoics focus on two vital things:

1. *How can one lead towards a happy and fulfilling life*
2. *How can one become a much better human being*

Stoicism's goals include attaining inner peace by overcoming adversities, being conscious of impulses, practicing self-care, realizing ephemeral nature as well as short allotted time. These are meditative practices which help them live with nature and not to be against them. It is highly imperative that individuals understand the challenges that they face and not turn their back on them. It is also crucial that they learn to transmute them to fuel that can feed their fire.

There are those individuals who share their favorite principles from Stoic School of Philosophy; the majority of them pertains to these thinkers. If fully embraced and regularly exercised, stoic tenets would champion one's creativity, facilitate workflow, and improve overall life and state of mind.

Creative works require individuals to be committed, vulnerable, courageous and adaptive and this also involves mindset which can negate distractions readily or even the negative impulses while they focus their minds and their hearts on what is essential. This is a challenging balancing act.

Without philosophy guiding life and work, individuals will succumb relentlessly to their distractions and excuses. Individuals sometimes make comfortable mistakes of acting on their moods and not on their principles.

- **_Accept that All Emotions are Coming from Within_**

In Meditations, Marcus Aurelius said that "_Today I escaped anxiety. Or no, I discarded it, because it was within me, in my perceptions — not outside._"

It's not the outside forces that make individuals feel something. It's actually what they tell themselves that create their feelings. A black canvass, document or unmarked to-do list isn't stressful. It is your thoughts that stress you out.

Many individuals wanted to place the responsibility, and the blame on external objects for the reason that it is easier to do but the fact remains that all the conflicts begin internally in the minds. When individuals flee from reality, an urgent mail, a deadline and more, they are doing nothing but harming themselves and discouraging their self-discipline. The moment you will come across an obstacle, and you feel resistance, do not look at things around you. Look within instead.

- **Find a Person You Respect and Use this Person to Stay Honest**

A letter from Seneca, a stoic includes and stated that: *"Choose someone whose way of life as well as words, and whose very face as mirroring the character that lies behind it, have won your approval. Be always pointing him out to yourself either as your guardian or as your model. This is a need, in my view, for someone as a standard against which our characters can measure themselves. Without a ruler to do it against you won't make the crooked straight."*

Taking, for instance, you are a writer and planning to start your own blog. Who would you look up to as your subject? There might be courses available around you, but you found out that they were irrelevant to your desires and aspirations. The good thing is that the internet now offers you access to amazing writers along with their admonishments, works, and stories. There will come a time that you would surely appreciate the value they offer, including their work platform, their ethics, and more that are worth learning from.

Regardless of what you do, be it drawing portraits, writing books, creating apps, making animation movies, and more, there are individuals that you can learn from. You are free to study their works, their stories, techniques, and even their failures and successes. You can also listen to interviews or reach out to them through sending emails. You can further discover patterns of success and then apply it into your life.

The thing that matters is realizing that it is not an act of comparison. If you do not get a book deal in five months or your product wasn't able to reach the top spot in the first weeks, this does not make you a failure. Instead, think of how you can learn from them. How are their principles and teachings help you learn, grow, and create? Everybody, regardless of how successful they are, there are mentors and heroes they look towards.

Realize that there is Life After Failures

"Does what's happened to keep you from acting with justice, generosity, self-control, sanity, prudence, honesty, humility, straightforwardness, and all other qualities that allow a person's nature to fulfill itself? So remember this principle when something threatens to cause you pain: the thing itself was no misfortune at all; to endure it and prevail is great good fortune." – Marcus Aurelius, Meditations

You can spend years on a particular project only for this project to be criticized and worst, completely ignored. There are undoubtedly instances where individuals worked on projects that they think would work well. They even spent years only to find out that a project is the most vulnerable work they have handled.

This is what failure can feel like when you are sharing a part of you. However, recovering from this failure is said to be a practice and a mindset. The lessons internalized from this experience is helping individuals do better works. This thinking goes like *"No failure, no growth."*

Stoic Wisdom that Helps in Cultivating Inner Peace

In 41 AD, Seneca was banished in Corsica Island by Emperor Claudio. Seneca spend his time in exile and take time to reflect on the nature of misfortune and human suffering mainly in the form of letters to family and friends.

These letters are rich in insights, both profound and practical to the nature of grief, anxiety, and suffering in general. But beyond all these, they recommend methods of cultivating attitudes and the minds so people may learn to face and combat their suffering and achieve inner peace within their distress. As per the words of Seneca, he stated that individuals should create serenity in the middle of the hurricane.

On Expectation

The biggest obstacle to living is an expectancy that hangs upon tomorrow, and this also tends to lose today. You're arranging those that lie in the Fortune Control and abandoning those that lie in yours. What are you searching for in life? What goal are you actually training? The entire future depends on uncertainty.

In most instances, individuals' decision and actions are guided by unseen beliefs, and mental scripts wherein expectations regarding the future are usually central. If individuals can identify and change these unacknowledged expectations, that usually take forms of negative talk. People stand better chances in following the advice of Seneca, and that is to take full responsibility for parts of their lives that they do not have control over and also to accept the part that they don't.

On Anxiety

Life is so short. This is anxious for individuals who forget the past and abandon the present and their fear for the future. They tend to dash from one pleasure to another and can't stay in just a single desire. They are losing the day because they are too busy waiting for the night and night in fearing the dawn. For psychologists working mainly with anxious individuals, it has been found out that avoidance is the root of anxiety which is taken by numerous individuals as constant distractions.

While distractions offer temporary relief, individuals pay the high price. Individuals' lives narrow and then constrict to the extent that they barely recognize themselves anymore.

On Friendships

Nothing delights a mind that much as loyal and fond friendship. However, you need to avoid individuals who are always lamenting and gloomy and those who often complain even about small things. Though the kindness and loyalty of a man might not be in doubt, someone who's groaning about almost anything and someone agitated is said to be enemy peace of mind. You might think that devotion and charity require unceasing tolerance of individuals in your life that fit the description of Seneca discussed above. But it is worth talking with a psychologist and asks yourself- even if you are more willing to sacrifice your peace of mind, what set of beliefs, attitudes, and behaviors about life, are you reinforcing through giving a willing ear to all those complains.

On Rest

Your mind should relax. It will rise keener and better if after rest. It sounds like not forcing a fertile farmland because the continuous activity will exhaust it eventually. Therefore, constant effort tends to sap your mental vigor while rest at the short period as well as relaxation will help in restoring your powers.

Since effort works most of the time, it is assumed that it must be applied in all given situations maximally. But as every stoic knows, blind application of efforts does not work out perfectly well.

Silphon phus

Chapter 5: Stoic Logic

For the ancients, logic generally includes anything remotely connected into rational thought. This is a messy and huge toolbox allowing individuals to make progress in the other two branches of philosophy known as ethics and physics.

The Stoic Logic-Essential Things You Need to Know

Stoic logic pertains to a system of propositional logic exclusively developed by stoic developers in ancient Greece. This is viewed to be one of the excellent logic systems in the classical world. Stoic logic is hugely shaped and built by Chrysippus; third head of Stoic school in third century BCE.

Chrysippus' logic differs from the term logic of Aristotle since this was based on proposition analysis instead of terms. The smallest unit in the stoic logic in assertible or proposition in stoic equivalent, this is the content of statement like "*it is the day*." The assertible can be established from simple ones to logical connective use. Resulting syllogistic is grounded on five standard indemonstrable arguments wherein all the other syllogisms are deemed reducible.

Towards the end of the days of yore Stoic rationale was ignored for Aristotle's logic. As a result, Stoic writings on rationale and logic didn't survive, and its main records were fragmented reports by different essayists and writers. Information about Stoic logic as one system was lost until the twentieth century.

This is what stoics are like in terms of logical matters, so they will be able to main that wise men are always dialectician. For all things is seen by means of considering arguments and what belongs to topics of ethics and physics.

The Stoics broadly contrasted logic with the wall that encompasses a field (it has been found out that ethics was considered the fruit and physics the land), or to eggshell (with ethics and physics inside)

In its expansive sense at that point, ancient logic incorporated all semantics, rhetoric, epistemology, logic, and grammar. Stoic logic involves quite a little bit, and some of this was ultimately influential in later thinkers.

Stoic rhetoric was the same as other types of classical rhetoric. They discussed forensic rhetoric invention, and more. However, the Stoics mainly emphasize brevity and clarity in style: stating precisely the only things necessary to get essential points over. They additionally stressed that moral and rhetoric character go hand in hand; you're not a "decent rhetorician" except if you are a "decent individual as well.

Stoic epistemology is rooted in "traditional language" or what is also called as "classical grammar." The Stoics were the main Westerners to offer names to things like verb forms, participles, articles, conjunctions, and adverbs-their vital contributions into Western grammar cannot be overstated.

Stoic epistemology is established in the possibility that all that everything individuals know eventually comes up through their five senses. Sense-Observation is the foundation of all learning. The senses can clearly lead individuals to go astray once in a while. However, the Stoics unendingly discussed how knowledge is conceivable with their incredible epistemological opponents, which are the Skeptics.

In any case, logic is taken in its modern and narrow sense, then the stoic logic-a system comprised of formal logical arrangements and reasoning created by highly prolific philosophers Chrysippus in the third century B.C.E. This is uncannily the same as the type of logic you find toward the start of initial rationale courses and textbook today. They were ahead of their comparatively radical time.

Nowadays, no one ultimately knows more about the syllogisms of Aristotle however, every digital circuit programmer, mathematician, computer programmer, and philosopher is very fluent when it comes to things that are close into stoic logic.

In present-day terms, what Stoics gave was an arrangement of natural deduction system that depends on five rules of inference. There are two sections into a system like this one: the inferences of rules acting upon them and propositions.

This is due to the very first full-fledged system of propositional logics that is closely relevant to modern Boolean logic. If ever you have taken a class in Artificial Intelligence, Mathematics and other classes that tackle general introduction into logic, then you have been exposed already into most components of the stoic logic.

Propositions

Unlike the more famous yet less powerful system of Aristotle that is based mainly on syllogisms, the stoic logic begins with plain propositions or statements that can be true or can be false. Favorite samples from ancient texts are:

- *Leo is walking.*

Here, complex propositions can be build up with the use of logical connectives. Ancient connectives look similar to the type of logic studied by many students today with certain light variations.

Conditional –If it's a day, it's light

Para conditional- Since it's a day, it's light

Disjunction-Either it's night, or it is a day

Conjunction-Both it's a day, and it's a night

Causal-Because it's a day, it's light

The less-It's less night than day

The more-It's more day than it's a night

Notice the stoic or is what's being called now as exclusive or. These days' convention of distinguishing between the two types carefully or did not develop until recently rather, therefore, disjunctions were rather confusing topics for the ancient students.

The Stoic Logic is perhaps one of the most imperative steps in the history of logic between Frege and Aristotle. It does not only have historical importance, but this is also worth reading as well as studying for due to its highly fascinating insights. Though the fragmentary state of evidence does not allow knowing all the refined details of their exclusive theory, some tutorials can present significant sources as well as alternative interpretations to provide ideas that are accurate as possible regarding the nature of the stoic logic.

Stoic logic covers a broad scope. Now, whether it pierces to whom individuals actually owe revival of Stoic logic or not, the certain thing is that from early decades of the 20th century, given the importance of developments in symbolic logic field, it has become more obvious that the stoic logic essentially differed from the Aristotelian logic and must be studied more on its own merits.

Chapter 6: Training of Perception

Some individuals may not know it, but in Stoicism, training of perception to avoid bad and good is a unique approach.

Stoics are known to have this exercise, which they referred to as Obstacle Upside Down. What they intend to do is make it impossible not to practice the art of philosophy. If you can turn the problem upside down properly, every bad problem can become a new source of good.

Suppose for a few seconds that you are trying to help somebody and their response was being unwilling to cooperate. Rather than making your life difficult, this exercise says they are leading you towards new virtues; as an example understanding and patience. Or it can be the death of someone dear to you so as your chance to express fortitude.

It is no bad or good at practicing stoic. There's just perception, and you can control perception. You can also choose to extrapolate your first past impressions; "This thing happened" or "This thing happened, and now it's over for me". If you would tie your very first response into dispassion, you will find out that everything is merely an opportunity.

Achieving Apatheia-Suggested Steps to Control Your Perception like a Real Stoic

The challenges people face in life make them emotional. The way people can overcome these challenges is to keep these emotions in proper check. Also, if they can keep steady regardless of the number of external events might fluctuate.

Ancient stoics have a word for this particular state, and that is apatheia. This pertains to a kind of calm equanimity which comes with the absence of irrational or even extreme emotions.

The following are the steps that you can take to attain this particular state, so you can concentrate more on overcoming obstacles instead of reacting on them.

Step 1-Steady Your Nerves

"What such a man needs is not courage but nerve control, cool-headedness. This he can only get by practice." — Theodore Roosevelt

---

During the Civil war, the troops were unloading the steamer when this exploded. Everybody hit the dirt but not Ulysses S. Grant, who runs towards the scene instead. This is nerve. Just like Grant, individuals need to prepare themselves for realities of their situations and keeping their nerves steady so that they can do their best.

Step 2-Take Control of Your Emotions

"Would you have a great empire? Rule over yourself."
— Publius Syrus

America sent their first astronaut in space, they have trained them in one important skill over the others, and that is the art of not panicking. Here on planet Earth, when anything goes wrong, people trade in their plans for the good emotional freakout. Real strength depends on the domestication of someone's emotions and not on pretending that they do not exist.

Step 3-Practice Objectivity

"Don't let the force of an impression when it first hit you knock you off your feet; say to it: Hold on a moment; let me see who you are and what you represent. Let me put you to the test." — Epictetus

In life, how many issues come and seem to originate from applying decisions to things we don't control? Discernments give people information regarding the precise moment when it's better to concentrate on what's instantly in front of them.

People should question their animalistic side or impulse to perceive what occurs quickly. Be that as it may, this requires strength and is a muscle that must be created.

Step 4-Contemptous Expressions should be Practiced

Stoics make use of contempt to expose things barely and strip away that legend which encrusts them.

Cooked meat is said to be a dead animal, and vintage wine is fermented and old grapes.

People can do this for anything that stands in their ways, considering things as they are, and not as that they have made them in our brains.

Step 5-Change Perspectives

"*Man does not simply exist but always decides what his existence will be, what he will become the next moment. Every human being has the freedom to change at any instant.*" — Viktor Frankl

Individuals need to keep in mind that they choose the way on how they look at things.

What they should do is limit and extend their point of view to whatever will keep them calmest and most prepared for the job that needs to be done.

Consider it selective editing which may include not to trick others, but to orient themselves instead appropriately.

Step 6-Live the Present Moment

"The trick to forgetting the big picture is to look at everything close up." — Chuck Palahniuk

It doesn't make a difference whether it's an awful time to be alive or the best, regardless of whether you're in a great job market or a terrible one.

What is important is right at this moment.

Concentrate on this moment and on what you can control at present. Not what might be or might not be ahead.

Step 7-Look for Opportunities

"A good person dyes events with his own color...and turns whatever happens to his own benefit." — Seneca

The fact of the matter is each circumstance, regardless of how negative, furnishes people with a positive, uncovered advantage they can follow up on if they only search for it.

Perhaps individuals were harmed just recently and are laid up in bed recouping. Presently they have sufficient energy and time to begin the book or the screenplay they have wanted to write.

That business choice that ended up being an error? Consider it to be a speculation that wasn't right. Like a researcher, you can gain from it and use it in your next trial.

Keep in mind: This a total flip. Seeing through negative, past its underside, and to its corollary, now that's positive.

Another method for putting it is to ask "Does being upset furnish you with more alternatives?

Now and then it does. However, in this very instance, it is assumed not.

Chapter 7: Stoicism in Growing Emotional Intelligence

There have been lots of writings about the significance of emotional intelligence lately. This is also known to play a vital role in Stoicism.

Emotional intelligence pertains to one's capacity to know about his or her feelings; to control and express them. It encourages a person to deal with his interpersonal relationships sympathetically and prudently. From various perspectives, emotional intelligence is the key to ultimate success in different aspects of life.

Understanding the real topics in Stoicism can help with the improvement of emotional intelligence. Stoicism is a way of thinking or a philosophy developed by famous philosophers namely Seneca, Epictetus and Marcus Aurelius

It was initially established by Zeno of Citium in the mid-third century BC and was vigorously impacted by Socrates. Stoicism is characterized as the capacity to suffer agony or hardship without grievances or any showcase of emotions. But, upon more profound investigation, one can locate some significant subjects in Stoicism that are related directly to the emotional intelligence of various people.

The core subject in Stoicism is to perceive what is under one's control. Stoics keep up that it is pointless to respond to things that they can't control. In sports, for instance, numerous factors are not constrained by the athletes. Relinquishing these and concentrating just on occasions or events that someone can control can be of great help.

Losing feelings on things that can't be controlled is debilitating and superfluous. Emotional energy, for example, outrage or anger, is better utilized when coordinated to controllable activities and actions. Athletes can undoubtedly improve their overall performance by not putting energy to waste just trying to change things that are beyond control.

Another significant standard of Stoicism is to comprehend one's feelings. This is critical to those into sports since games can be enthusiastic from various perspectives. Feelings are brought about by numerous occasions and can shift rapidly. Now and then, mastering someone's feelings is as simple as understanding and getting them.

Mastery of emotions or feelings does not mean living with no emotions. It implies that sentiments like displeasure and pity won't be lost on things that individuals can't control. It additionally means that individuals figure out how to replace negative emotions with positive feelings like contentment and calmness.

Individuals frequently baffled when they attempt to control things, yet when they let go of this serious need for control, they can encounter more delight and joy. That is, by making an effort not to control what they can't control, they figure out how to control what they can control.

Stoicism's final principle centers on fitting in with the real world and the reality of life. So as to make the best out everything, one must have a sensible viewpoint. Defining reasonable objectives and desires is fundamental, and attempting to make reality to adjust to your wants is vain. It bodes well to adjust your desires to the real world.

At last, Stoics make the best out of each circumstance, even misfortune and catastrophe. They generally observe the lessons and exercises to be learned, and essential moves and actions to be made. They locate the newest opportunities in all things. This is how winners are ultimately born.

Chapter 8: Learn More about Stoic Ethics

The enormous impact Stoicism has applied on a moral idea from early Christianity through Immanuel Kant and into the twentieth century is once in a while comprehended and much more seldom valued. Since the beginning, Stoic moral and ethical doctrines have both incited harsh actions and have inspired more enthusiastic defenders.

The Stoics characterized the objective in life as living in concurrence with nature. People, in contrast to every other creature, are comprised naturally to make reason as real adults, which change their comprehension of themselves and their actual goodness. The Stoics also stated that virtue is the only genuine good, and both are important. In contrary to Aristotle, this is enough for happiness and no way that it depends solely on luck.

Life's virtue is free all passions, which are inherently exasperating and hurtful to the spirit and soul. Yet, it incorporates the right emotive responses molded by normal comprehension and fulfillment of all a person's civic, professional, social and personal responsibilities. The Stoics believed that the individual who has accomplished ideal consistency in the task of his rational resources, the "wise man," is amazingly rare, yet fills in as a prescriptive perfect for all. The Stoics also believed that advancement toward this honorable objective is both vitally urgent and possible.

Meaning of End

Stoicism is widely known as the eudaimonistic hypothesis, which implies that the zenith of human undertaking or 'end' or telos is eudaimonia, which means all-around flourishing or happiness. The Stoics characterized this end as "living in concurrence with nature." "Nature" is said to be a multivalent and complex idea for Stoics. Thus their definition of the objective or the final end of the human striving is ultimately rich.

The principal sense of such definition is living in complementary with nature in general, for example, the whole cosmos or universe. The cosmic nature, which is known as the universe, Stoics strongly believed is well-ordered and rationally organized system. It is coextensive indeed with Zeus will be known as the impersonal god. Thus, all events that happen within the universe fit inside a well-structured and coherent scheme, which is also providential. Since there's no room for chances within the rationally organized system, the metaphysical determinism of the stoics dictated further that this enormous nature is indistinguishable from destiny. In this way and at this level, "living in concurrence with nature" signifies adjusting one's will with the arrangement or sequence of events that are destined to happen in the soundly established universe, as fortunately willed by Zeus. Each thing within the universe has its very own particular character and constitution. This second sense of nature is the thing that individuals use when they state it is the nature of fire significantly moves upward. The way where living things become, change, and die recognizes them from how non-living things become, change as well as cease to be.

The nature of the plants is very distinct from the nature of sand and rocks. To "live in concurrence with nature" in this subsequent sense would, therefore, incorporate, for instance, metabolic functions: taking in growth, development, nutrition, reproduction as well as ousting waste. A plant that is effective at in carrying out is a flourishing and healthy specimen. Aside from basic metabolism, animals do have capacities of desire, locomotion and sense of perception.

Additionally, creatures have an intrinsic motivation to think about their offspring. Hence living in concurrence with the animality of a creature includes more mind-boggling practices than those of a plant living in concurrence with its nature. For an animal parent to disregard its own offspring would accordingly be for it to act in contrary to its temperament or nature.

Stoics believed that as compared to different creatures, people are neither the most grounded, nor the quickest, nor the most amazing swimmers, nor able and ready to fly. Instead, the unmistakable and unique human limit is the reason. In this manner for individuals, "living in concurrence with nature" signifies living complementarily with their extraordinary, intrinsic endowment-the capacity to reason.

Appropriation Theory

Stoics have developed an advanced psychological theory to clarify how the coming of reason on a fundamental level changes the world perspective on people as they develop and mature. This is the appropriation theory or oikeiôsis, a specialized term which researchers have likewise interpreted differently as affiliation, affinity, familiarization and orientation.

The word implies the acknowledgment of something as one's own, as having a place with oneself. Something contrary to oikeiôsis is allotriôsis, a term that flawlessly translates to a word known as "alienation." Based on the theory of Stoic regarding appropriation, there are two diverse formative stages. In the main stage, the intrinsic and initial impulse of a living creature, plant, or animal is self-love and not pleasure, as the opponent Epicureans battle. Organisms know about their constitution. However, for plants, this awareness is said to be more primitive than it is for the animal creatures. This mindfulness includes the prompt acknowledgment of its own body as "having a place with" itself. The animal is in this way, coordinated toward keeping up its constitution on its proper and natural condition.

As a consequence, the organism is affected to save itself by seeking after things that promote its very own wellbeing and by staying away from things unsafe to it. Pleasure is just the result of success in this action. On account of a human newborn child, for instance, appropriation clarifies why the infant looks for his mother's milk. As the child matures, his constitution tends to evolve.

The child keeps on cherishing himself, yet as he develops into youthfulness, his ability for a reason rises and what he perceives as his constitution, or self, is critically changed. Where he recently distinguished his constitution as his body, he recognizes his constitution rather with his intellectual capacity (reason) in a specific connection to his body.

So, the self that he presently adores is his rationality. The human reason gives individuals the affinity with cosmic reasons, nature, that aides the universe. The completely developed adults, therefore, come to distinguish his genuine self, his actual great, with his developed and idealized rational soul. This ideal condition of the discerning soul is what virtue is. While the initial phase of the appropriation theory gives a record of relationship toward one's self, the subsequent stage clarifies social relationship toward others. The Stoics have observed that parents are typically incited to cherishing their kids, and worry for their welfare.

Parental love is inspired by the intimate affinity of the child and the likeness to her. Be that as it may, there are reasons that may be common or nearly similar to another individual. People recognize themselves with their own close or immediate family. However, with all members of the human race, they are all kindred individuals from the more extensive rational community. Along these lines, the Stoics implied social appropriation to comprise explanation of the natural genesis of altruism.

The Good, the Evil, and the Indifferent

The Stoics characterized the good as "what is finished according to the nature for rational being qua discerning being. As clarified over, the idealized nature of a rational being is decisively the flawlessness of reason, and the perfection of this reason is a virtue.

The Stoics maintained dubiously among antiquated ethical idea that the main thing that consistently adds to happiness, as its vital and adequate condition is also virtue. Alternately, the main thing that requires bad or evil or it can also be misery is the defilement of reason, vice to be specific.

Every other thing was judged neither evil nor good, yet rather fell into the class of "indifferent." They were classified as such because the Stoics held that these things in themselves, neither adding to nor bringing down a happy life. Their indifference is neither harm nor benefit since this can be utilized badly and well. Be that as it may, within the class of indifference, the Stoics recognized the "preferred" from "dispreferred." The third subclass contains the 'outright' indifference. For example, regardless of whether the quantity of hairs on one's head is odd or it's even, whether to twist or expand one's finger. The preferred indifferent are said to be according to nature. On the other hand, dispreferred indifferent is in contrary to nature.

This is on the grounds that use and possession of the favored indifferent usually promotes the normal state of an individual, thus choosing them is generally complemented by reason. The favored indifferent incorporate life, wellbeing, delight, excellence, quality, riches, great notoriety, and honorable birth. The preferred indifferent incorporate health, beauty, pleasure, good reputation, noble birth, wealth, strength and life. Dispreferred indifferent include ignorable birth, low repute, poverty, weakness, ugliness, pain, disease and death.

While it is typically suitable to maintain a strategic distance from dispreferred indifferent, in strange conditions, it might be ethical to choose them instead of staying away from them. The virtue or vice of the specialist is decided not by the ownership of an impassive, yet rather by how it is utilized or chosen. It is the idealistic utilization of indifference that fulfills a real and happy existence and the horrible use that makes it miserable.

The Stoics expounded a point by point taxonomy of virtue, isolating ethicality into four fundamental types, namely moderation, courage, justice and wisdom. Wisdom is said to be subdivided into quick-wittedness, good sense, discretion, good calculation and resourcefulness. Justice is also subdivided to fair dealing, equity, and honesty.

Moreover, courage is subdivided to industriousness, cheerfulness, high-mindedness, confidence and endurance. Moderation is also subdivided to seemliness, self-control, modesty and good discipline. Stoics similarly divide the vice into injustice, intemperance, foolishness and the likes.

The Stoics further kept up that virtues are entailing between involving and establish a solidarity which implies to have one is actually to have them all. They held that same virtuous mind is moderate, just, courageous and wise. Therefore, a virtuous individual is someone disposed of in a particular way concerning every individual virtue.

In order to support the doctrine of the unity of the virtue, stoics provided an analogy just as somebody is both orator and poet and general yet still an individual so as the virtues are unified. However, applied into different action spheres.

Perfect Acts and Appropriate Acts

When an individual has created reason, he actually can perform proper functions and acts. The Stoics characterized a proper action as a reason that persuades a person to do, or that person admits reasonable justification. Maintaining good health is a good example.

Since health and wellbeing are neither great nor terrible in itself, but instead is fit for being utilized well or maybe poorly used, opting to maintain one's good health, for instance, walking and other acts or exercises that go in harmony with the action of the agent.

This is on the grounds that the specialist must have the right comprehension of the activities he performs. In particular, his choices and dismissals must form a constant arrangement of activities that is reliable with the majority of the virtues at the same time. Every single deed speaks to the harmony and totality of his ethical or moral integrity.

Most individuals are non-virtuous because, although they may pursue reason effectively in honoring their parents, they neglect to conform to "the laws of life" in general by acting suitably with respect to the majority of different ideals and virtues.

The scale of the activities from vicious into virtues can be spread out are as follows:

(1) Actions performed "against appropriate act," which incorporate disregarding one's folks, not treating companions and friends kindly, not acting devotedly, and wasting one's wealth on the wrong situations and conditions;

(2) Intermediate suitable activities in which the operator's manner and disposition aren't reasonably predictable and consistent, thus would not consider idealistic, despite the fact that the activity itself approximates the right conduct.

Samples include honoring the parents, the siblings and the nation, associating with companions, and giving up one's riches in the right conditions. The "perfect acts" performed in the correct path by the specialist with an entirely consistent, rational and perfect disposition and the latter is referred to as virtue.

Passions

As many individuals have seen, only the virtue is good, and this is choice-worthy as well, and just it's contrary, which is vice, that is terrible and to be wholly avoided based on the stoic ethics. By far, most of the individuals neglect to get this. Ordinary individuals routinely and wrongly judge different events and objects to be great and bad, which is, in fact, indifferent. Disposition in making judgment somewhat disobedient to reasons is a psychic disturbance at which stoics referred to as passion or pathos.

Since passion is considered impulse (the soul's movement) which is unreasonable and in spite of reason, it contrary and irrational to nature. The four common types of passion are pleasure, appetite, fear and distress. Pleasure and distress pertain to present appetite, objects and fear to future objects.

Distress or misery is an unreasonable compression of the soul differently portrayed as malice, jealousy, envy, vexation, anguish, annoyance, sorrow, worry, pity and grief. Fear is the shrinking of soul irrationally and an expectation of something terrible, which may include agony, hesitation, shame, shock, terror, dread, superstition and panic.

Appetite can be defined as the irrational swelling or stretching of the soul that reaches for the expected good. This is also referred to as yearning, want, quarrelsomeness, hatred, intense sexual desire or spiritedness and wrath. Pleasure can also be a silly delight over what seems like worth choosing; it incorporates cheering at another's enchantment, misfortunes, rapture and self-gratification.

The virtuous person's soul had interestingly had 3 of great states or the full of feeling reactions, also known as the eupatheiai. The 3 good states of the soul include wishing joy and caution. Joy is the opposite of pleasure is sensible elation. Good spirits, enjoyment, and tranquillity are classified under this.

Caution is the opposite of fear, and this is reasonable avoidance. Sanctity and respect are sub-types of caution. The opposite of the appetite is wish and also a valid striving and described as goodwill as well as contentment, acceptance and kindliness. There are no such good feelings that are contrary to the passion of distress.

Take, for instance, the virtuous individual encounters bliss in the organization of one particular friend. However, perceives that presence of that friend isn't itself a genuine virtue yet just preferred. In other words, the organization of his friend is to be looked for in as much as doing even the slightest work does not in any way includes any awful acts like a neglect of his obligations to other people. The companion's absence doesn't hurt the spirit of the virtuous individual, just the vice does.

The soul of the virtuous individual is grasped by the enthusiasm of joy and pleasure in the presence of wealth. At the point when the riches are lost, this silly judgment will be replaced by the irrational judgment that corresponds and that poverty is seriously bad, making a vicious individual miserable.

Thus, the virtuous individual wishes to see his companion only during the course of events, and it is a great idea to happen. His desire is in this manner is reserved (hupexhairesis): You wish to see your friend if it's fated and if Zeus really wills it. If the event does not occur, then a virtuous person isn't thwarted, and this results in being unhappy and disappointed.

His desire is objective and in concurrence with nature, both in the feeling of being respectful to the reason (which is unmistakable of the human constitution) and in the feeling of being in harmony with the many different events in this world.

The virtuous individual isn't indifferent in the sense of being cruel like a statue. Or maybe, he carefully recognizes what really creates a difference into his bliss or happiness- vice and virtue from what doesn't. This reliable and firm understanding keeps the good and bad times of his life from turning into the clairvoyant aggravations or "pathologies" the Stoics tend to understood passions to be.

CPSIA information can be obtained
at www.ICGtesting.com
Printed in the USA
LVHW082241130221
679115LV00008B/622